Drupal Development Tricks for Designers

Designers

Dani Nordin

O'REILLY®

Beijing · Cambridge · Farnham · Köln · Sebastopol · Tokyo

Drupal Development Tricks for Designers
by Dani Nordin

Published by O'Reilly Media, Inc., 1005 Gravenstein Highway North, Sebastopol, CA 95472.

O'Reilly books may be purchased for educational, business, or sales promotional use. Online editions are also available for most titles (*http://my.safaribooksonline.com*). For more information, contact our corporate/institutional sales department: (800) 998-9938 or *corporate@oreilly.com*.

Editors: Julie Steele and Meghan Blanchette	**Cover Designer:** Karen Montgomery
Production Editor: Melanie Yarbrough	**Interior Designer:** David Futato
	Illustrator: Robert Romano

Revision History for the First Edition:
    2012-03-16   First release
See *http://oreilly.com/catalog/errata.csp?isbn=9781449305536* for release details.

ISBN: 978-1-449-30553-6

[LSI]

1331825607

Table of Contents

Part I. Setting Up a Local Development Environment

Preface

In the first guide, *Planning and Managing Drupal Projects*, we walked through the process of planning a site, figuring out the user experience, and working with content architecture. In the second, *Design and Prototyping in Drupal*, we started looking at how to create solid, user-centered design that works for a Drupal site, and how to allow Drupal's default behavior to guide your design decisions without defaulting to making a site look "Drupally."

In this guide, *Drupal Development Tricks for Designers*, we start looking at just a little bit of real, honest-to-goodness, developer Ninja Magick. I'm going to share what I've learned over years of building Drupal sites about setting up a development environment, getting yourself ready to collaborate on code with others, and other ways to make site building easier so you can focus on design.

Wait, What? Why?

I realize the idea of learning how to use the command line, or set up a local development environment, isn't as sexy as learning how to push the envelope of Drupal design. Trust me, I get it. But if there's one thing that prevents Drupal designers from pushing that envelope, it's this: *site building in Drupal isn't as efficient if you haven't figured out at least a few of these tricks.* Want to know why the same task takes some developers an hour or two, while it takes some of us several hours of banging our heads against the computer? It's because they know how to quickly update their modules, or how to use version control (hallelujah!) to protect themselves from bonehead mistakes.

The goal of this guide isn't to show you everything that you can possibly do to make development easier for yourself, or to provide a comprehensive guide to everything a given development tool can do; the list is entirely too long, and if you're anything like me, you'll get halfway down the list before you start wondering where your coffee is and forget you ever looked at it. My goal here is simple: *to help you figure out how much of this stuff you need to make repetitive tasks in Drupal take less time.* The rest, you can figure out once you get the hang of it.

A Note for Windows Users

As you read through these pages, you might note that the instructions I provide here are focused on the Mac platform. Although I don't want to ignore my friends on Windows, most of what I've learned about working with Drupal—particularly the command line stuff—simply works more efficiently on the Mac platform. Unfortunately, Windows adds a rather annoying layer of complexity to most of the command line stuff that you'll see in these pages. Dear friends in the community have tried several times to work in Git and Drush on Windows, and all have fought with their machines for hours on end to get their configurations running. This complexity has led many of the developers I know to forgo Windows altogether and get things done on Mac or Ubuntu.

If you do, however, prefer Windows, you can use a program like Cygwin to create a UNIX-like environment on your PC; or if you're feeling adventurous, a program like VirtualBox will allow you to install a Linux distribution such as Ubuntu directly on your machine, which you can then use as a virtual machine to work on command line stuff. If you're planning on Drush (see Chapter 3 for several reasons why you darn well should), there's actually a Drush for Windows installer, which you can download at *http://drush.org/drush_windows_installer*.

The Designer's Coding Toolkit

Every Drupal designer and developer has their own set of preferred applications for making their work easier; the following is a list of applications I personally use, and that many of my friends in the Drupal community also prefer. If you've got something to add to this list, I'd love to hear it! Leave a comment on the website: *http://drupalfor designersbook.com*.

MAMP

MAMP creates a virtual Apache server directly on your Mac. Using it, you can prototype, build and theme a Drupal site quickly on your local machine, without having to worry about FTP servers, or people accidentally seeing your half-finished work. If you're working independently, or your staging server is incredibly slow, the time savings of working locally can not be understated. Working locally is also a beautiful thing when you don't have Internet access, or access is spotty; I once got a website halfway to launch on a plane ride to Texas.

Dropbox

Dropbox allows you to manage files across the Internet using a folder on your desktop. The glory of Dropbox is that it's free (for up to 2GB), it works on any platform, and it allows you to access your files on any machine that has Dropbox installed. I keep my MAMP site files in a folder within my Dropbox, which allows me to work on sites from wherever I happen to be, no matter which computer I'm working on. The one challenge to the Dropbox/MAMP combination is where databases are stored; although you can easily store your site files in a Dropbox folder, the database files exist on whatever machine you're on, which means that you have to sync the databases from one machine to the other if you want to do work on a different machine. This can be done using a program like Navicat (see "Navicat" on page vii) or exporting the updated database and using the export file to restore the database on your other machine. The Backup and Migrate module (*http://drupal.org/project/backup_migrate/*) makes this process relatively easy.

Coda

I first mentioned Coda in *Design and Prototyping for Drupal*, but it's worth mentioning again. Coda is a relatively inexpensive (under $100) application for coding websites. Not only does it allow you to code your pages and upload them in the same screen, it also has the ability to connect to Terminal on your remote server from within the application, which is useful when you're running shell commands, like Drush or Git. Most importantly, Coda's Clips library allows you to keep commonly used code snippets in one place and insert them into your HTML simply by double-clicking. This is extraordinarily useful in theming; I keep CSS3 snippets and Drupal theme hooks in the Clips library, so I can add them to my template files at any time.

Terminal

Terminal is a native application in Mac OS X that lets you run command-line prompts. If you're going to use Git or Drush, you will need to get cozy with Terminal.

Navicat

Navicat is a Mac-based application that helps you manage databases. While you can also use PHPmyAdmin (which comes with MAMP), what I like about using Navicat is that it's highly visually oriented, and you can connect—in one location—not just to databases on your local hosting environment, but on other hosting environments as well, as long as you've set up a way to access the host remotely. As hosting companies tend to deal with remote access differently, make sure you check your hosting company's FAQ or support wiki for how to establish remote access. With Dreamhost, which I use, it's generally as simple as entering the IP address you're trying to access the host from into an "allowed hosts" field in the user's profile.

Git

Git is a free, open source version control system. It allows you to not only keep separate versions of your work, it allows you to revert to an old version of your work should you make a change and everything breaks. This is particularly important when doing custom work, such as theming or building a custom module, or when upgrading modules, as relatively minor things can sometimes cause everything to go haywire in your Drupal installation. Check out Chapter 4 for more info on using and installing Git in your development environment.

Drush

Drush is a shell program you can install on any server with a Drupal installation, including your local development environment, which allows you to access several key tasks from the command line. Why do this? Because once you get the hang of it, it takes significantly less time to do many key tasks (like syncing databases, installing or updating modules, and clearing caches). We'll go deeper into the awesomeness that is Drush in Chapter 3.

From the Trenches: Ben Buckman

Ben Buckman is a Drupal developer currently living in Buenos Aires, Argentina. His shop, New Leaf Digital, specializes in helping Drupal teams solve tough development problems. He is also a co-founder of Antiques Near Me, a web-based startup (built in Drupal!) that helps connect antique collectors with shops and events near them.

Dani: You've always been very generous in terms of showing me how to do things in Drush, Git, etc. What made you want to help me? Obviously, development stuff is your gig, so what's the benefit to passing this kind of knowledge along to non-developers?

There are probably many motivations, the most rational one being, it's a win-win. It's not a threat to me if designers know Git; in fact, it makes it easier to work with them. (As long as I keep learning new things, I'll always be 10 steps ahead of the people I'm teaching with the things I know better, and they'll be 10 steps ahead in the things they know better, and that makes for a good market/community/etc.) Proprietary knowledge is short-sighted; there's plenty of work to go around. It also makes me a go-to resource for development questions, which has all sorts of practical benefits. If I said, "I know how to do that but I won't tell you," people would think I was a jerk and not want to work with me, and if no one knew that I knew anything, they wouldn't know to refer clients to me.

Dani: In terms of what you've shown me directly, you've gotten me started with Drush and Git, and I think I sort of ended up spiraling from there into learning Drush Make and Install Profiles. Are there any other developer-centric tools that you think designers could benefit from?

Learn other shell tools like `grep`, `find`, `tail -f`, piping, loops, and writing shell scripts, and the power is endless. You can dump text to your clipboard on a Mac by piping to `pbcopy`. You can have the terminal tell you via Growl when a DNS record has propagated. Or write a deployment script to push your code, ssh to the server, and pull it, that you call with one line. The UNIX shell is like a pocket toolkit; once you know how each tool works (and they're usually simple on their own), you start to see all kinds of problems as easily solved with a few commands.

[Author's note: I have no idea what he just said.]

Other than that...Firebug or the Webkit (Chrome/Safari) Inspector has made web development much easier. Everyone should know how to test CSS and JavaScript in the inspector so they don't have to keep saving-reloading-saving-reloading.

Dani: What do you think designers can gain from using these tools?

Efficiency...proficiency...People should know the things they work with. We should all know the basics of how a car works, if we drive a car. Likewise if we use a computer, or build things that work across networks of computers, we should know the basics of how they work. (And the UNIX shell happens to be a good way of getting straight to the raw underbelly of all these systems.) Developers should know their way around a Photoshop file, and designers should know their way around Git and bash and some PHP, and we'll all understand each other better.

Dani: In terms of workflow management, I know that one of the things that you like as a developer is being able to solve interesting problems in Drupal (or whatever technology you're using for the product). Where do you think the balance should lie? What's the ideal engagement for you—building the whole thing from scratch, or consulting during the early phases of a project and then helping the design team put together the more advanced functionality?

This is a good question, and I can't say I've found the perfect balance. I've covered a pretty wide range in the last few years. Lately I've been building some websites from start (static designs) to finish (site in production) and I don't usually enjoy those projects. The challenges (basic content architecture) are mostly repetitive, and the clients don't understand the difference between a good product and a bad one half the time. Too much of the emotional value of those projects depends on the quality of the client—a bad client makes those projects awful from start to finish, whereas a truly interesting project can be rewarding even if the client is unpleasant.

The ideal engagement for me is working with designers or site builders who hit a glass ceiling in their development skill sets and want a boost up, or developers who want another brain to help think out of the box. Everyone should know what they don't know and be able to reach out to people to fill those gaps. If I teach someone to fish on a project, they might not need me on the next project, but they'll very likely refer me to someone else who does. I like doing custom development on existing sites, or refactoring bad code (when the client understands what they're asking for). A client recently wanted functionality added to some existing but partially built modules to bridge Webform with contextual filters in Views, with the resulting code submitted as a patch for the community to use; I really like that kind of project. I also like doing investigative troubleshooting. Aside from client work (and a separate startup business I co-founded), I enjoy learning new platforms, and have been spending a lot of time lately immersed in Node.js.

Dani: In your mind, at what point in the project does it make sense to hire a developer, and at what point should a designer or site builder be able to figure things out on their own?

The point where your budget justifies hiring some additional help. ;) Actually, this is probably a better question for you to answer than me, since I'm on the other side of the equation. I know that I'd pay someone to teach me the inner workings of Varnish, because I've hit a wall with what I can learn by Googling. I'm often amazed what non-developers can build with Drupal, but eventually if you want something out of the box, you'll need to write some code, and most designers don't write modules. (Different side of the brain? I don't know.) Also I've written about a trend in Drupal toward higher complexity, which brings more bugs, which means it's more likely you'll need a developer to troubleshoot something.

Conventions Used in This Book

The following typographical conventions are used in this book:

Italic
> Indicates new terms, URLs, email addresses, filenames, and file extensions.

`Constant width`
> Used for program listings, as well as within paragraphs to refer to program elements such as variable or function names, databases, data types, environment variables, statements, and keywords.

`Constant width bold`
> Shows commands or other text that should be typed literally by the user.

`Constant width italic`
> Shows text that should be replaced with user-supplied values or by values determined by context.

 This icon signifies a tip, suggestion, or general note.

 This icon indicates a warning or caution.

Using Code Examples

This book is here to help you get your job done. In general, you may use the code in this book in your programs and documentation. You do not need to contact us for permission unless you're reproducing a significant portion of the code. For example, writing a program that uses several chunks of code from this book does not require permission. Selling or distributing a CD-ROM of examples from O'Reilly books does require permission. Answering a question by citing this book and quoting example code does not require permission. Incorporating a significant amount of example code from this book into your product's documentation does require permission.

We appreciate, but do not require, attribution. An attribution usually includes the title, author, publisher, and ISBN. For example: "*Drupal Development Tricks for Designers* by Dani Nordin (O'Reilly). Copyright 2012 O'Reilly Media, Inc., 978-1-449-30553-6."

If you feel your use of code examples falls outside fair use or the permission given above, feel free to contact us at *permissions@oreilly.com*.

Safari® Books Online

 Safari Books Online (*http://my.safaribooksonline.com*) is an on-demand digital library that delivers expert content in both book and video form from the world's leading authors in technology and business. Technology professionals, software developers, web designers, and business and creative professionals use Safari Books Online as their primary resource for research, problem solving, learning, and certification training.

Safari Books Online offers a range of product mixes and pricing programs for organizations, government agencies, and individuals. Subscribers have access to thousands of books, training videos, and prepublication manuscripts in one fully searchable database from publishers like O'Reilly Media, Prentice Hall Professional, Addison-Wesley Professional, Microsoft Press, Sams, Que, Peachpit Press, Focal Press, Cisco Press, John Wiley & Sons, Syngress, Morgan Kaufmann, IBM Redbooks, Packt, Adobe Press, FT Press, Apress, Manning, New Riders, McGraw-Hill, Jones & Bartlett, Course Technology, and dozens more. For more information about Safari Books Online, please visit us online.

How to Contact Us

Please address comments and questions concerning this book to the publisher:

O'Reilly Media, Inc.
1005 Gravenstein Highway North
Sebastopol, CA 95472
800-998-9938 (in the United States or Canada)
707-829-0515 (international or local)
707-829-0104 (fax)

We have a web page for this book, where we list errata, examples, and any additional information. You can access this page at:

http://www.oreilly.com/catalog/9781449305536

To comment or ask technical questions about this book, send email to:

> *bookquestions@oreilly.com*

For more information about our books, courses, conferences, and news, see our website at *http://www.oreilly.com*.

Find us on Facebook: *http://facebook.com/oreilly*

Follow us on Twitter: *http://twitter.com/oreillymedia*

Watch us on YouTube: *http://www.youtube.com/oreillymedia*

Acknowledgments

To be honest, I'm still amazed at being given the chance to write this book. It had been swirling around in my mind for a while, and I consider it one of life's happier coincidences that I happened to get the opportunity to write about Drupal in not one, but two major books this year.

A brief list of thanks to the folks who have helped me in various capacities to help this book see the light of day:

My intrepid editors, Julie Steele and Meghan Blanchette, for giving me the opportunity to write the book, and for helping me make sense of O'Reilly's lengthy style guide. Also thanks to Laurel Ruma for making the introduction to Julie so I could actually *sell* this crazy idea.

Todd Nienkerk of Four Kitchens (*fourkitchens.com*) helped me understand how the ideas I've used in really tiny teams apply to the work of larger teams; his feedback as a reviewer (as indicated by the many times I quote him throughout this text) was invaluable.

Ben Buckman of New Leaf Digital (*newleafdigital.com*) is one of the main reasons I know any of this stuff in the first place, and was kind enough to lend a developer's eye to the text—including kindly nudging me about my consistent misuse of *Master* and *Origin* in the Git chapter.

Jenifer Tidwell, a local UI Designer, was also kind enough to review this book and provide perspective from a designer who doesn't know Drupal. If you haven't read her book *Designing User Interfaces* (another O'Reilly Title), you should.

Various colleagues and professional acquaintances, in and out of the Drupal community, who were kind enough to let me interview them for this series: Ben Buckman of New Leaf Digital, Greg Segall of OnePica, Richard Banfield of Fresh Tilled Soil, David Rondeau of inContext Design, Todd Nienkerk, Jason Pamental, Amy Seals, Mike Rohde, Ryan Parsley, LeisaReichelt, and Andrew Burcin.

Claudio Luis Vera, for introducing me to Drupal and being a mentor, collaborator, and commiserator for the last several years. Also, Ben Buckman of New Leaf Digital, who has been one of the guiding forces behind my passion to bring Drupally knowledge—particularly Drush, Git, and other stuff—to my fellow designers.

Finally, I want to thank the niecelet, Patience Marie Nordin, for giving me someone to be a role model to, and my husband, Nicolas Malyska, for being the most supportive partner anyone can hope for.

About the Reviewers

Todd Ross Nienkerk, Four Kitchens co-founder, has been involved in the web design and publishing industries since 1996. As an active member of the Drupal community, Todd regularly speaks at Drupal events and participates in code sprints all over the world. As a member of the Drupal.org Redesign Team, Todd helped spearhead the effort to redesign Drupal.org and communicate a fresher, more effective Drupal brand. He is also a member of the Drupal Documentation Team and has chaired tracks for DrupalCon Copenhagen 2010, DrupalCon Chicago 2011, DrupalCon Denver 2012, and DrupalConMunich 2012. Todd is currently serving as the DrupalCon global chair for all design, user experience, and theming tracks.

Jenifer Tidwell has been designing and building user interfaces for a variety of industry verticals for nearly two decades. She has experience in designing both desktop and web applications, and currently designs and develops websites for small businesses. She recently worked on redesigning the interface for Google Books. Before that, as a user interface designer at The MathWorks, Jenifer was instrumental in a redesign of the charting and visualization UI of MATLAB, which is used by researchers, students, and engineers worldwide to develop cars, planes, proteins, and theories about the universe. Jenifer blogs about UI patterns and other design-related topics at *http://designinginter faces.com/blog*.

Ben Buckman started programming with the BASIC page in a kids' magazine, and has been building websites since 1995. In college, he studied political philosophy and worked as a web developer. Today, his shop New Leaf Digital (*http://newleafdigital .com/*) specializes in development and assistance for non-developers with the Drupal content management system, and development with the Node.js platform. Ben has also ridden a motorcycle across 35 US states, loves to sail, and is a co-founder of Antiques-NearMe.com. He currently lives in Buenos Aires.

Setting Up a Local
Development Environment

CHAPTER 1

Setting Up a Local Development Environment and Installing Drupal

When I first started working in Drupal, I created all my sites on a staging URL (like newsite.tzk-design.com) that lived as a subdomain of my studio website. Updating a module meant downloading the project from drupal.org, unpacking and uploading it to the staging URL, then running updates manually on the server. Theming meant making changes to a file, uploading it to the server, and refreshing the page to see changes.

While this is a totally reasonable way to work, there were a few problems with it:

- Depending on my Internet connection or the size of a file, uploading files to a server took a significant amount of time—particularly when you add up the time spent tweaking little bits of CSS and checking the results.

- If I had no Internet connection (for example, when traveling), or the connection was spotty, I was screwed.

- Perhaps most importantly, *everything I was doing could conceivably be found by someone else on the Web.* This left me constantly worried that people—particularly clients—would end up randomly finding my half-finished work all over the Web. And while there were certainly ways to avoid that, like HTTP authentication on the server[1], that alone didn't solve the first two problems, which are much more annoying.

When I finally figured out how to set up a local hosting environment on my laptop (thanks to a few wonderful friends in the Drupal community, including developer Ben

---

1. If you are using a remote staging server, one way to prevent your dev/staging environments from being seen is to edit the *.htaccess* file (included in Drupal) to require all visitors to use a password just to view the site. You can use this tool to create the text you need to paste into the top of *.htaccess*: *http://www .htaccesstools.com/htaccess-authentication/*. Then use this to generate the *.htpasswd* file that contains the username and password: *http://www.htaccesstools.com/htpasswd-generator/*. Of course, I didn't learn any of this until *after* I'd discovered how to work locally, but that's my issue, not yours.

Buckman, interviewed earlier), I was delighted. Now I could develop sites more efficiently from anywhere I happened to be with my laptop. Of course, it also meant that I was more likely to work on vacation (ask me about the time I had to launch a website in the middle of a yoga retreat), but overall, it's been very worth it.

In this section, we'll focus on creating a local development environment, and installing Drupal 7 in a temporary folder we can access from that environment. In later chapters, we'll learn a bit about the command line, install Drush and use it to download and enable some modules, and learn how to set up Git so we can keep track of changes and revert mistakes easily. Before we start, we have to install MAMP.[2] Once you download the software package, simply drag the MAMP folder into your Applications folder and drag the icon into your dock for easy access.

Step 1: Install MAMP

In order to set up a Drupal-friendly environment on your computer, you'll need an Apache server running PHP version 5 and MySQL. The good news is that you can get this—easily and for FREE—on the Web (see Figure 1-1). If you're on the Mac platform, you can download MAMP at *http://mamp.info* for free.[3]

Once you have your copy of MAMP downloaded, you'll want to set up your computer to support development on your local server (which is called *localhost*).

Step 2: Setting Up Your Main File Structure

Drupal's database and code depends on having a well-organized file structure. MAMP, and its Windows and Linux counterparts, essentially turn a single folder in your computer into a miniature development server. This means that all of the sites you develop in MAMP will be subfolders of that main folder (e.g. */MAMP/my-crazy-awesome-site*). Once you have MAMP installed, it's important to make sure you set the location of the main folder to something that makes sense for your filesystem, and to back up that folder regularly. I like to keep my MAMP folder in a Dropbox (*http://getdropbox* *.com*), which allows me to sync my site files in the cloud and access them from any computer I'm on.

---

2. If you want to try some other options, there's also XAMPP, which is open source and available for a host of systems, including Windows, OS X, and Ubuntu.

3. If you're on Windows, you can download WAMP at *http://www.wampserver.com*. If you're on Ubuntu, the Lullabots have put together a video on how to install a LAMP server on Ubuntu: *http://www.lullabot* *.com/videos/install-local-web-server-ubuntu*.

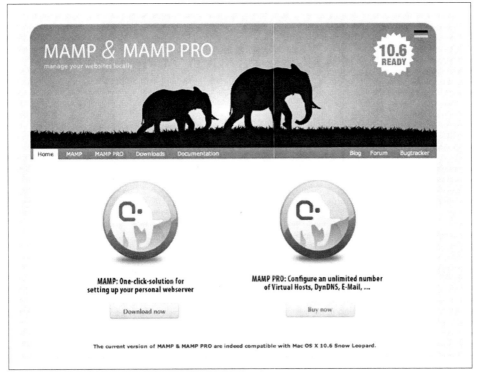

Figure 1-1. Screenshot of mamp.info. You want the one on the left.

To start up MAMP and reset the main folder's location:

1. After you've installed MAMP and moved the application icon into your dock, press the MAMP icon in your dock. This will start up the MySQL server and PHP. You should see a screen like the one in Figure 1-2.

2. Ignore the browser window that it opens up and go back to the MAMP application.

 If you want to turn off the Start screen, you can change it in your MAMP settings by unchecking "Open start page at startup" from the Start/Stop tab in the Preferences screen.

3. Choose Preferences from the menu on the right, and go to the Apache Tab (see Figure 1-3). Set the document root (which we'll call the "web root" going forward) to something that makes sense for your filesystem (see Figure 1-3). As I mentioned earlier, I'm using a Dropbox for my files.

Figure 1-2. The MAMP application screen

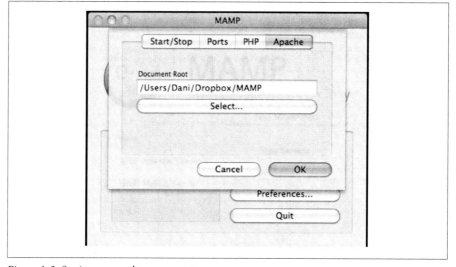

Figure 1-3. Setting up our document root

 When starting up MAMP for the first time, you may get a dialog asking you if you want to use MAMP or MAMP Pro. If you get this dialog, choose MAMP instead of MAMP Pro. For most Drupal development, the free version of MAMP will be more than sufficient.

Dropbox is available at getdropbox.com, and it allows you to store up to 2GB of data for free, which is synced over the Web. If you don't have a ton of large files to store, it's an easy way to keep your data available to you no matter what machine you're on. If you build sites using multiple machines, however, you also need to make sure to sync your databases among those machines; MAMP keeps the databases you create in the */Applications/MAMP/db/mysql* folder of the machine you create them on, so you may have to export a file of the site's database using a module like Backup and Migrate (drupal.org/project/backup_migrate), and import them into the database of the machine you're working on at the beginning of each session. Backup and Migrate lets you back up your site's database and import databases from other sources; it also includes Dropbox integration, which allows you to export the databases directly into a Dropbox instead of on the FTP server.

Step 3: Setting Up the Drupal files

Drupal's core files are hosted as a project on Drupal.org along with thousands of contributed modules (called "projects") that can extend the core functionality of Drupal. Start the installation process by downloading Drupal at drupal.org/project/drupal. You want to download the *latest stable release* of Drupal 7 (7.12 as of this writing).

Once you have these files downloaded, extract the Drupal folder into your MAMP directory, and rename the folder to something that makes sense for your site. I like to name my site folders after the client, generally using a short code for them to save time when navigating to the site. For example, my portfolio site, tzk-design.com, is in my MAMP folder as */tzk*. For this demonstration, we'll be using the folder name *d7-demo*.

 It is essential that any code that you add to or customize for your Drupal site—whether it's modules, themes, or uploaded files—goes into the */sites/* folder, and not into any of the core folders, e.g. the core *modules* or *themes* folder. Not doing this could result in all your hard work being replaced the next time you upgrade. Seriously.[4]

Now that you've extracted Drupal and put it into your MAMP directory, navigate to the *sites* folder within your Drupal files. Any modules, themes, libraries, etc. that you use to customize this Drupal site should be downloaded into the *sites/all* folder, in folders named *modules, themes,* or *libraries*, depending on their purpose. If you're using Drush to download modules (which we'll be doing in Chapter 3), Drush will create those folders within the *sites* folder for you if they don't exist. Because it's awesome.

Now, to develop locally, we want to create a *localhost* folder within *sites,* which will hold the database settings for our local Drupal installation. If you're already cozy with the command line, there are several ways you could set this up, including creating multiple local sites within the same Drupal installation; however, for our purposes, we can stick with creating a *localhost* folder.[5] Once you've created that folder, navigate into the *sites/default* folder and make a copy of the file called *default.settings.php*, move

---

4. All. Of. It.

5. If you plan on using the same Drupal distribution to host multiple sites (which is totally valid and possible), you'll need to learn how to create multiple local URLs.

it into your *localhost* folder, and rename the file to **settings.php**. Leave it alone for now; you'll need it for what happens later.

You may notice that we're putting our Drupal configuration in a different folder than *sites/default*, which is the typical way of installing Drupal. We're doing this because leaving *sites/default* where it is for now is useful for minimizing confusion when you eventually publish the site to its final URL. Doing this, however, means that all the changes you make in your Drupal site will be stored in the *localhost* folder, and you will need to use `drushsql-sync` to sync the *localhost* database with the *default* database, which will require logging into the staging server via SSH. You can also sync the local and remote databases using a program like Navicat (see "Step 4: Creating the Database" on page 8), or by exporting the *localhost* database and importing it into the remote site—both of which can be done using the Backup and Migrate module (*drupal.org/project/backup_migrate*). As with all things in Drupal, there are about 372 ways to accomplish the same goal.

Step 4: Creating the Database

Drupal stores all the information related to your site in a database. In order to install Drupal, you need to create this database on your local MySQL server.

You can create a database using phpMyAdmin, which is free and comes with MAMP (instructions on how to create the database using phpMyAdmin are available in "Using phpMyAdmin" on page 10). If you prefer a more visually oriented way of dealing with databases, Navicat, a paid software package available at navicat.com, is one of the best programs I've found. Although the premium software is on the pricey side (and you'll need it for copying or syncing databases on multiple servers, unless you use `drushsql-sync`—important when it's time to launch your site), you can download an inexpensive version called Navicat Premium Essentials for about $10 at www.navicat.com/en/download/download.html. Both are available for Windows, Mac, and Ubuntu. If you just want to check it out for now, you can also download Navicat as a free trial for 30 days.

For the purposes of this demonstration, we'll use Navicat Premium. The process in Navicat Premium Essentials should basically be the same.

1. Open Navicat and select Connection→New Connection→MySQL from the top menu.

2. Create your settings as shown in Figure 1-4. Your hostname is *localhost*, and your username and password will both be *root*. Port, if you've left your MAMP defaults as is, will likely be *8888*. Mine has been changed to *8889*, for reasons I can't remember.

Figure 1-4. Connection settings in Navicat for our local MAMP server.

3. Once you've created the connection, open the connection by double-clicking its name in the left column. Right-click on the connection name and select "Create New Database" from the menu (see Figure 1-5). Give the database a name that represents the project you're creating; I'm going to call this one *d7-demo*.

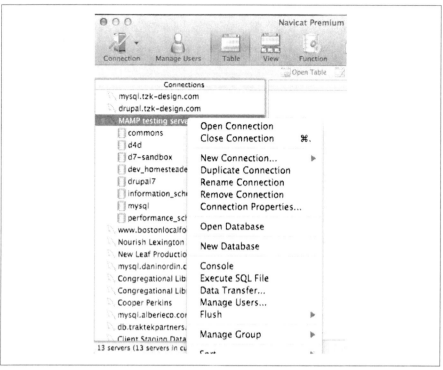

Figure 1-5. Right-clicking your server in Navicat gives you a handy contextual menu that'll let you perform key database operations.

That's it. Done. See how easy?

Using phpMyAdmin

If you decide that you'd rather just stick with phpMyAdmin to create your database, you can start that journey by clicking the "Open Start Page" on your MAMP home screen (see Figure 1-6).

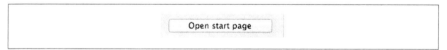

Figure 1-6. The "Open Start Page" button will take you to your MAMP homepage, where you can access PHPMyAdmin.

Once you get to the MAMP Homepage, you'll see a tiny link under the "MySQL" heading that will take you to phpMyAdmin. Clicking that link will take you to the phpMyAdmin interface, where you can create a database simply by typing a name into the "Create New Database" field (see Figure 1-7). Again, we'll call this one *d7-demo*.

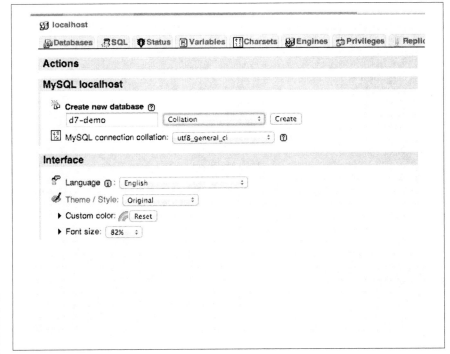

Figure 1-7. Creating a new Database is pretty easy in PHPMyAdmin.

The new database you create will come set up with all the privileges your *localhost* user needs to install Drupal. When it comes time to transfer the database from your local server to a staging or production server, you'll need a new database with different permissions—but that's for another time. For now, we press onward.

Step 5: Install Drupal

Now that you've created your database, go back into your favorite browser (I use Chrome: *http://www.google.com/chrome*) and go to *localhost:8888/d7-demo/install.php*. Choose the "standard" installation profile for now (see Figure 1-8); it will take care of some basic configurations for you. On the next page, select English as the installation language. If you need to install it in another language, there's a handy link on that screen that will show you how to do it.

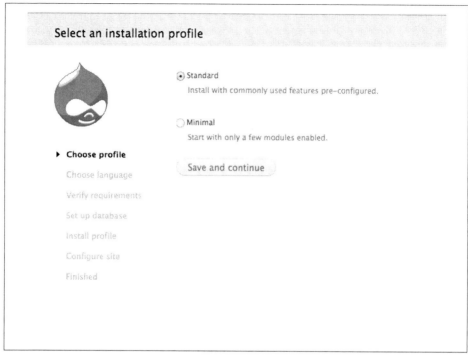

Figure 1-8. Choosing the "Standard" profile when installing Drupal will set you up with some basic functionality for your Drupal site.

Now that you've taken care of that, it's time to add the values for the database that we just created. On the screen that follows, enter the values that you provided when you created the database. In my case, the database name is *d7-demo*, the host is *localhost*, and the username and password are both *root*.

You might be wondering why we're setting up Drupal with a pretty obviously insecure password. When you're developing locally, security is important, but less of an issue than when you're developing on a remote site. When you transfer this local version of the site to a remote server, for staging or production, you're actually going to create a new database (with a stronger username and password), and sync the data from the local database to the new remote database.

Submit the form, and Drupal will install itself within a couple of minutes. When the installer finishes (see Figure 1-9), you'll be able to fill in some basic site details along with a username and email address for the administrative user account.

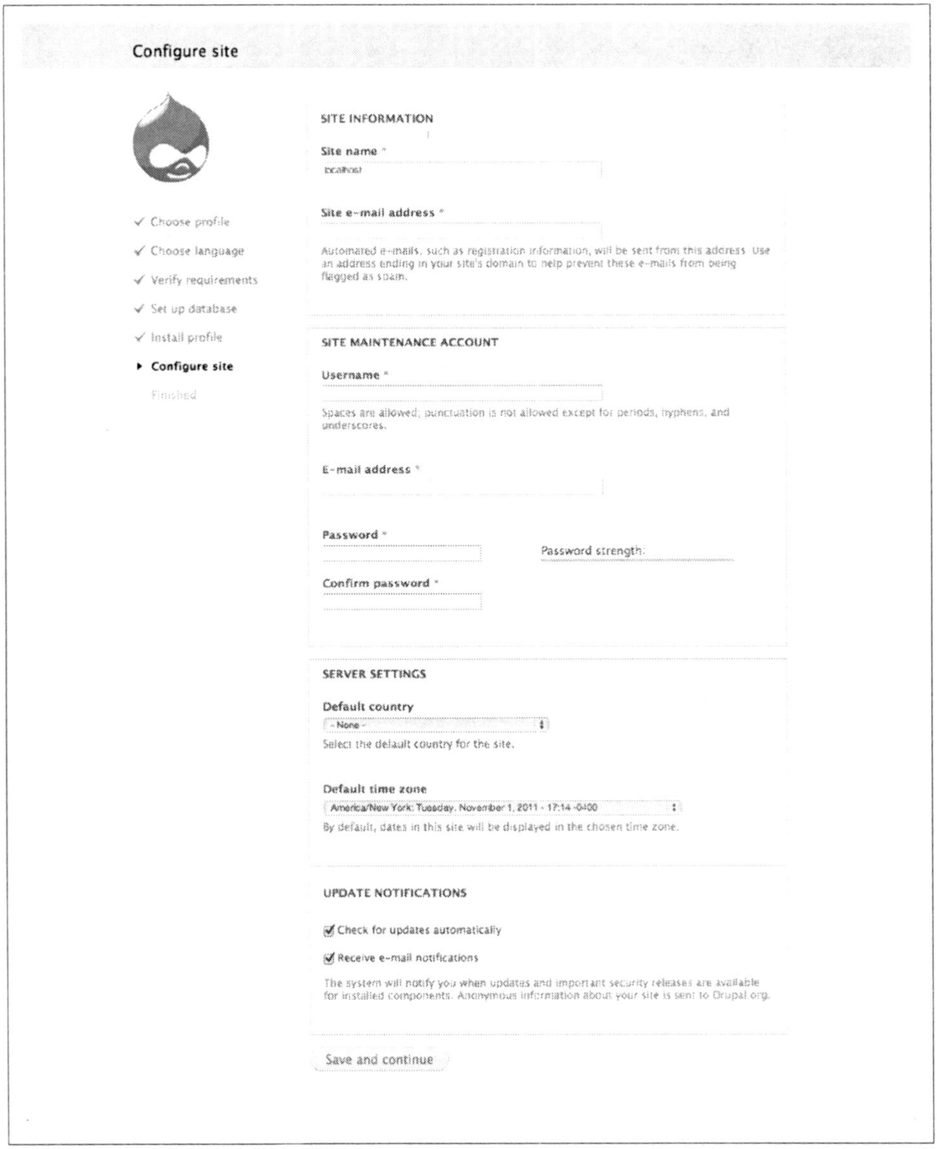

Configure site

SITE INFORMATION

Site name *

localhost

Site e-mail address *

✓ Choose profile
✓ Choose language
✓ Verify requirements
✓ Set up database
✓ Install profile
▶ **Configure site**
Finished

Automated e-mails, such as registration information, will be sent from this address. Use
an address ending in your site's domain to help prevent these e-mails from being
flagged as spam.

SITE MAINTENANCE ACCOUNT

Username *

Spaces are allowed; punctuation is not allowed except for periods, hyphens, and
underscores.

E-mail address *

Password *   Password strength:

Confirm password *

SERVER SETTINGS

Default country

- None -   ▼

Select the default country for the site.

Default time zone

America/New York: Tuesday, November 1, 2011 - 17:14 -0400   ▼

By default, dates in this site will be displayed in the chosen time zone.

UPDATE NOTIFICATIONS

☑ Check for updates automatically

☑ Receive e-mail notifications

The system will notify you when updates and important security releases are available
for installed components. Anonymous information about your site is sent to Drupal.org.

Save and continue

Figure 1-9. Once you've installed Drupal, you can set up some of the site's initial configuration.

The first user created in the installation process is given permission to do everything on the site, ALWAYS. Therefore, it is strongly advised never to use this user as your own personal account, but rather as an administrator account, and to give it a strong password. The site might be just on your computer now, but when you move it online, you'll need to make sure to preserve the user accounts. Drupal requires all email addresses for site users to be unique, so if you have only one email address, it makes sense to create a second email account, like *admin.user@gmail.com*, that you use specifically for the administrator account. For some email providers, like Gmail, you can also add a "+" to the email address to create a subaccount. Drupal 7 will recognize these as a separate address, e.g. *dani+drupaladmin@gmail.com* will go to *dani@gmail.com*.

Congratulations! You now have an empty Drupal site, ready for content. Before we start playing with Drupal, however, it's time to move on to a few more things that can make local Drupal development easier. Next up, we'll learn just a little bit of the command line to prepare us to start working with Drush, which will help us more efficiently download and update modules and themes.

CHAPTER 2

Working on the Command Line: Some Basic Commands

Okay, folks, here we are: it's time to start looking at the command line. Back when I was a young and naïve Drupal designer, I fought passionately against the command line, arguing that Drupal should be easy enough that I shouldn't *need* to use Terminal to get things done. And technically, many aspects of Drupal are easy enough to get away without needing it. But, my friend, *easy* (or rather, easy-ish) doesn't mean *efficient*. Since then, I've made a point of learning just enough command line to get by.

Here's why you should use the command line:

- **It's quicker.**   Many commands are just a few characters, and can get you to what you need to be doing in half the time of ordinary methods. When we get into Drush in Chapter 3, you'll see this firsthand.

- **It makes you feel like a ninja.**   Let's face it: even with all the wonderful usability enhancements that have been built into Drupal 7, working in Drupal can be intimidating for people who aren't developers by training. Being able to work in the command line, just a little bit, can be ridiculously gratifying.

- **It makes developers like you.**   While I've certainly annoyed my share of developers by asking them constant questions about different command-line things, the majority of the developers I've spoken to genuinely appreciate someone who's willing to learn the basics. For one thing, it makes their jobs easier (no constant asking for minor things while they're trying to solve complex code issues); for another, it helps give you a common language.

Commands

Here's a super-quick primer on command-line things you should know. Use them in good health.

 Some of these commands are a bit scary and can mess up your filesystem if you're not careful. Make sure to use these commands with caution, and keep backups of your work. Luckily, we'll be talking about backups when we get to working with Git in Chapter 4.

~

This character (technically called a *tilde*; I usually call it *squiggly*) is your HOME folder. On a Mac, this is usually located in *Macintosh HD/Users/YOURNAME*.

cd

Use this command to navigate to a particular directory in your filesystem. If you want to navigate to your MAMP folder, for example (assuming that, like mine, it's located inside a Dropbox folder), you'd use the command cd ~/Dropbox/MAMP.

ls

This command will list the contents of any folder you're in.

mkdir

This command will make a directory in whatever folder you happen to be in.

mv *FILENAME DESTINATION*

This command will move the file you specify into the destination you specify. It's also useful for renaming a file.

chmod

Use this command to modify permissions on a file or folder in a system. This command can be configured in any number of different ways, and frankly, it can be pretty confusing. With the exception of using it to make Drush executable when I install it on a server (see Chapter 3), I rarely use it.[1]

rm *FILENAME*

This command will remove any file you specify. Use this with EXTREME CAUTION; removing files willy-nilly can mess up your system.

rsync -a *SOURCE DESTINATION*

This command, one of my favorites, will sync two folders of your choice. It's easiest to use when the two folders you're syncing are in the same main folder; for example, if you have a staging site on a subdomain of your main site, e.g. Staging.site.com and site.com, you could use the code rsync -a staging.site.com/ site.com/ from

---

1. There is, however, a pretty decent rundown of this command on Wikipedia, should you be feeling brave today: *http://en.wikipedia.org/wiki/Chmod*.

your web root to sync the files—in far less time than you would need to copy them via FTP.

 Make sure you include the trailing slashes in your URLs, which ensures that you're copying the *contents* of the folders and not the folders themselves.

That Wasn't So Bad, Was It?

Now that we've got that over with, it's time to start looking at Drush. Ready? I knew you would be.

CHAPTER 3

Installing Drush

Drush is the Drupal Shell, a mighty library of commands that are designed to make your life easier in Drupal. Among the many things you can do with Drush, some of the most exciting (from a designer/site builder's standpoint) are:

- `drush dl module_name`: Download any module from drupal.org. You can even download a string of modules by separating the names with spaces.
- `drush en module_name`: Enable any of the modules that you just downloaded. Like dl, you can enable a string of modules by typing a space-separated list.
- `drush up`: This is my single favorite thing to use Drush for, and the reason that you, dear reader, MUST LEARN DRUSH. With this simple command, you can update all of your modules and Drupal core in about five minutes, as opposed to the— *ahem*—considerably longer amount of time it takes to do it manually.

If you'd like to see a demonstration of the merits of using Drush versus installing modules manually, check out the video "More Beer, less effort" from Development Seed: *http://developmentseed.org/blog/2009/jun/19/drush-more-beer-less-effort/*. Synopsis: installing a site and a pile of modules via Drush versus manually left our hero with an extra hour or more of time on his hands—plenty of time to celebrate with a frosty beverage.

Installing Drush

Grab the Drush package from drupal.org/project/drush. You want to download the *tar.gz* file containing the latest recommended release (see Figure 3-1).

 You can also go to *http://www.drush.org/resources* to find a bunch of resources related to Drush, including a handy Windows installer, for those dear readers who work on a PC.

Drush

View   Version control

Posted by moshe weitzman on *November 13, 2006 at 2:00am*

drush is a command line shell and scripting interface for Drupal, a veritable Swiss Army knife designed to make life easier for those of us who spend some of our working hours hacking away at the command prompt.

See http://drush.ws, the homepage for the drush project. It contains many important resources for drush users.

It is valid to use the latest '7.x' (or master) no matter what your version of Drupal is. Drush is independent of Drupal version :)

drush is not a module, and does not participate in the usage statistics system at drupal.org.

A list of modules that include Drush integration.

Beloved Windows users. Please use the All-versions-5.x-dev release. There is a convenient Drush installer for Windows available on drush.ws. The 4.x releases are not at all Windows compatible.

Drush was originally developed by Arto for Drupal 4.7 (this alpha code can still be found in the DRUPAL-4-7 branch). In May 2007, it was partly rewritten and redesigned for Drupal 5 by frando. The module is now maintained by Moshe Weitzman, Owen Barton, Adrian Rossouw, greg.1.anderson, jonhattan, and Mark Sonnabaum.

#D7CX: I pledge that Drush will have a full Drupal 7 release on the day that Drupal 7 is released.

Downloads

Recommended releases

Version	Downloads	Date	Links
7.x-4.4	tar.gz (247.08 KB) | zip (289.47 KB)	2011-Mar-14	Notes

Figure 3-1. The Drush project page. You can download the recommended release of any project by clicking the "tar.gz" link.

Unpack the *tar.gz* file into your working folder. If you're developing locally, this could be the *Users/USERNAME* folder; if you're on a remote server (and you have shell access—this is important), you would unpack it into the directory OUTSIDE the folder that holds the site's public files.

 Drush works inside any directory that contains a working Drupal installation. If you've hosted multiple sites on the same server, you can install Drush once on the main server, and use it by navigating (via the command cd ~/*path/to/directory*) to the directory that contains the site you want to work with.

Once you have Drush unpacked, you want to make the Drush file executable. You can do this by using the following code:

```
chmod u+x /path/to/drush
```

Where */path/to/drush* is the location of your Drush folder (in my case, this is ~/drush/drush). Once you've done that, you want to create an *alias* to Drush so you can use the command outside of the actual Drush folder, e.g. your various Drupal installations. This is where things get interesting, but it's only for a moment.

You'll start by entering the following code:

```
nano ~/.bash_profile
```

This opens an old-school text editor that will allow you to create an alias to Drush, giving you the ability to run Drush commands from within any folder that contains a Drupal installation. There might be one or two lines of code here, but you don't need to worry about those. Scroll down and make sure you're on a new line at the end of the file, and add the following code:

```
alias drush='PATH/TO/DRUSH'
```

So on my computer, it looks like Figure 3-2.

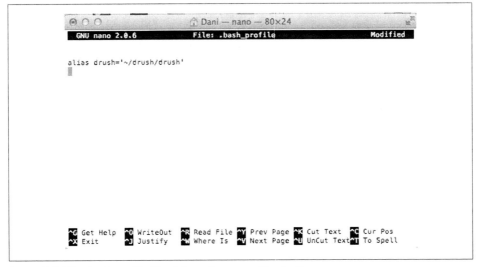

Figure 3-2. The .bash_profile file with our fancy new Drush alias.

Save the file using <control>-x, y (for yes) and <enter>.

If you're interested in learning just a bit more command line, Jenifer Tidwell, a UI designer from the Boston area, also suggests this one line trick to adding a line to your *.bash_profile*. Be careful to enter the text EXACTLY AS SHOWN, or you'll have to go into a text editor anyway.

```
% cat >> ~/.bash_profile alias drush='PATH/TO/DRUSH'
# click ENTER
^D
# click CTRL+D
```

Once you've finished updating your *.bash_profile*, type the following:

```
source .bash_profile
```

to reload your updated *.bash_profile*. Now, if you type **drush**, you should see something like Figure 3-3.

```
Danielles-MacBook-Air:~ Dani$ source .bash_profile
Danielles-MacBook-Air:~ Dani$ drush
Execute a drush command. Run `drush help [command]` to view command-specific
help.  Run `drush topic` to read even more documentation.

Global options (see `drush topic core-global-options` for the full list):
  -r <path>, --root=<path>              Drupal root directory to use
                                        (default: current directory)
  -l http://example.com,                URI of the drupal site to use (only
  --uri=http://example.com              needed in multisite environments)
  -v, --verbose                         Display extra information about the
                                        command.
  -d, --debug                           Display even more information,
                                        including internal messages.
  -y, --yes                             Assume 'yes' as answer to all
                                        prompts
  -n, --no                              Assume 'no' as answer to all prompts
  -s, --simulate                        Simulate all relevant actions (don't
                                        actually change the system)
  -p, --pipe                            Emit a compact representation of the
                                        command for scripting.
  -h, --help                            This help system.
  --version                             Show drush version.
  --php                                 The absolute path to your PHP
                                        intepreter, if not 'php' in the
                                        path.


Core drush commands: (core)
  cache-clear (cc)      Clear a specific cache, or all drupal caches.
  core-cli (cli)        Enter a new shell optimized for drush use.
  core-cron (cron)      Run all cron hooks in all active modules for specified
                        site.
  core-rsync (rsync)    Rsync the Drupal tree to/from another server using ssh.
  core-status (status,  Provides a birds-eye view of the current Drupal
  st)                   installation, if any.
  core-topic (topic)    Read detailed documentation on a given topic.
  drupal-directory      Return path to a given module/theme directory.
  (dd)
  help                  Print this help message. See `drush help help` for more
                        options.
  image-flush           Flush all derived images for a given style.
  php-eval (eval, ev)   Evaluate arbitrary php code after bootstrapping Drupal
                        (if available).
  php-script (scr)      Run php script(s).
```

Figure 3-3. Look at all the fancy!

Another Option: Creating a Symbolic Link to Drush

Todd Nienkerk, of Austin's Four Kitchens, also recommends this method for skipping the old-school text editors (nano, vim, etc.) by creating a symbolic link using the command:

```
ln -s /PATH/TO/drush/drush /usr/local/bin/drush
```

Then close and reopen Terminal. Type **which drush** to verify that it's installed; if it gives you the path /usr/local/bin/drush, you're done.

Note that the second "drush" in */PATH/TO/drush/drush* is IMPORTANT. In the example I've described, my literal command would be:

```
ln -s ~/drush/drush /usr/local/bin/drush
```

Now the Fun Begins

Now that you have Drush installed, there are all sorts of things you can do from the main folder of any working Drupal installation:

- Need to download and enable a module? Type `drush dl` *MODULE_NAME*, where *MODULE_NAME* is what comes after drupal.org/project/ in the URL.
- Need to update some modules? Type `drush up`. What used to take a few hours if you had a lot of modules to update, now takes a few seconds.
- Clear the caches? `drush cc all`.
- Enable a new module? `drush en` MODULE_NAME.

It's just so beautiful!

Putting This in Action: Installing Modules

Want to start playing with Drush? Let's go back to our D7 Demo site. Once you've installed Drush, open Terminal and navigate to the *d7-demo* folder using the command `cd ~/Dropbox/MAMP/d7-demo`. Again, this assumes that you've set up your MAMP folder inside a Dropbox folder; if you haven't, the path will be wherever your *d7-demo* folder is located on your system.

Now that we're in there, we're going to start downloading some modules. For this project, we'll start with a few basic modules:

Pathauto and Token
> Modules that help you automatically create sensible URLs for your site's content.

Views and CTools
> Modules that help create dynamic lists of content on your site. I've heard that it's possible to have a Drupal site that doesn't require the Views module; however, I have yet to see one.

Block Class
> Allows you to add custom classes to individual blocks. This is very useful for theming.

Link
> Allows you to create Link fields.

Media
> Allows you to create fields to accommodate a variety of media, including video uploads, sharing from YouTube, etc.

Devel

This module gives you some quick links to help during development, including letting you generate placeholder content—very useful if you're trying to prototype quickly.

For now, we'll stick with Bartik, the theme that comes pre-installed with Drupal 7. If, however, we wanted to download a new base theme along with these modules, we could do that as well, and Drush would install the theme in */sites/all/themes*.

To download our modules, we would enter the following into Terminal (remember, we're in our *d7-demo* folder):

```
drush dl pathauto token views ctools block_class link media devel
```

Click Enter, and you'll see something like what's in Figure 3-4.

```
Danielles-MacBook-Air:~ Dani$ cd Dropbox/MAMP/d7-demo
Danielles-MacBook-Air:d7-demo Dani$ drush dl pathauto token views
 ctools block_class link media devel
Project pathauto (7.x-1.0) downloaded to
 [success]
/Users/Dani/Dropbox/MAMP/d7-demo/sites/all/modules/pathauto.
Project token (7.x-1.0-beta7) downloaded to
 [success]
/Users/Dani/Dropbox/MAMP/d7-demo/sites/all/modules/token.
Project views (7.x-3.0-rc3) downloaded to
 [success]
/Users/Dani/Dropbox/MAMP/d7-demo/sites/all/modules/views.
Project views contains 2 modules: views, views_ui.
Project ctools (7.x-1.0-rc1) downloaded to
 [success]
/Users/Dani/Dropbox/MAMP/d7-demo/sites/all/modules/ctools.
Project ctools contains 9 modules: views_content, stylizer, page_
manager, ctools_plugin_example, ctools_custom_content, ctools_aja
x_sample, ctools_access_ruleset, bulk_export, ctools.
Project block_class (7.x-1.0) downloaded to
 [success]
/Users/Dani/Dropbox/MAMP/d7-demo/sites/all/modules/block_class.
Project link (7.x-1.0) downloaded to
 [success]
/Users/Dani/Dropbox/MAMP/d7-demo/sites/all/modules/link.
Project media (7.x-1.0-rc2) downloaded to
 [success]
/Users/Dani/Dropbox/MAMP/d7-demo/sites/all/modules/media.
Project media contains 3 modules: media_internet, file_entity, me
dia.
Project devel (7.x-1.2) downloaded to
 [success]
/Users/Dani/Dropbox/MAMP/d7-demo/sites/all/modules/devel.
Project devel contains 3 modules: devel_generate, devel, devel_no
de_access.
Danielles-MacBook-Air:d7-demo Dani$ ▌
```

Figure 3-4. Drush downloads all of the modules that we ask it to into the sites/all/modules folder. Total time? About 30 seconds.

Now, we can enable the modules that we need—either by checking them off in the Modules screen (*admin/modules*), or through Drush by adding the code drush en mod ule_name. Let's try the latter. Enter the following code:

```
drush en views views_ui ctools media media_internet file_entity devel devel_generate
link block_class pathauto token
```

and press Enter. You should get something along the lines of Figure 3-5.

```
Danielles-MacBook-Air:~ Dani$ cd Dropbox/MAMP/d7-demo
Danielles-MacBook-Air:d7-demo Dani$ drush en views views_ui ctools media media_i
nternet file_entity devel devel_generate link block_class pathauto token
devel is already enabled.                                          [ok]
link is already enabled.                                           [ok]
The following extensions will be enabled: views, views_ui, ctools, media, media_
internet, file_entity, devel_generate, block_class, pathauto, token
Do you really want to continue? (y/n): y
block_class was enabled successfully.                              [ok]
ctools was enabled successfully.                                   [ok]
devel_generate was enabled successfully.                           [ok]
file_entity was enabled successfully.                              [ok]
media was enabled successfully.                                    [ok]
media_internet was enabled successfully.                           [ok]
token was enabled successfully.                                    [ok]
views_ui was enabled successfully.                                 [ok]
pathauto was enabled successfully.                                 [ok]
views was enabled successfully.                                    [ok]
FirePHP has been exported via svn to                          [success]
/Users/Dani/Dropbox/MAMP/d7-demo/sites/all/modules/devel/FirePHPCore.
Danielles-MacBook-Air:d7-demo Dani$
```

Figure 3-5. Enabling all of our modules through Drush. Total time? About a minute.

 When doing certain things in Drush, you may end up with an error saying that you've exceeded your memory limit. If this happens, I often fix it by going into *sites/default/settings.php* and adding the code `ini_set('memory_limit', '128M');` to the file. Do a search for the term "ini_set" in the text and put the code at the top of all those values.

You may have to change the permissions on *settings.php* in order to change the file; make sure that you set it back to 444 when you're done. This ensures that once you've made your changes, nobody else can change your file—particularly important when the site is live. Drush also has its own settings file, *drushrc.php*, which you can adjust in order to give Drush more memory while keeping Drupal's memory at a reasonable limit.

So now, in about five minutes, we've done what it would have taken us over an hour to do manually. This, dear reader, is why you should learn Drush.

Now that we've gotten used to the command line, and we've started downloading and enabling modules on our *d7-demo* site, we need to make sure that we can back up our work. For that, we'll need to learn Git, the open source version control system.

CHAPTER 4

Getting Started with Version Control

The reasons for using version control on your Drupal projects are several and various, and have only recently become clear to me as I've started working with Drush and Git. Although adding version control to your workflow can be daunting at first, the benefits far outweigh the initial annoyances. Consider this:

- In a recent project, while attempting to theme complex navigation on a Drupal 7 prototype, I found myself messing things up in a bad, bad way, shortly before stakeholders were supposed to look at the site. Because we had Git installed on our server, I was able to roll back to the former, not messed-up menu and leave it there while we focused on other priorities—without having to make a frantic phone call to our developer.

- When working with more than one person, especially on remote teams, version control allows you not only to figure out who made what changes to the code, it allows you to work on the same file at once without accidentally overwriting each other's changes.

- Finally, version control also ensures you have exactly the same files installed in all locations. This means that you never have to worry that your local site is on a different version of a module than your server copy.

 If you don't have a GitHub account yet, skip to "Step 4: Set Up a GitHub Account" on page 33 for a moment and come back.

In this chapter, we'll install Git in our local development environment, set up a local and remote repository for our *d7-demo* site, and learn how to work Git into our Drupal workflow.

Master Versus Origin

Git allows for multiple development tracks to be going on simultaneously, using a technique called branching. Branches could be used to separate work by multiple developers on a team, to isolate work on specific bugs, or to separate development code from stable/production code. Working with branches is not necessary to get started with an effective version control workflow, however; so for now, we'll assume all work is on the default branch, called "master." Where the word "master" appears in the Git commands to follow, you can substitute other branch names if you're using other branches.[1]

When working with Git, you'll primarily be working with a local copy, or clone, of your repository (which we'll be calling *Master*) and pushing/pulling that copy to a remote copy, called *Origin*, usually hosted on a separate server. A *repository*, in version control terms, is a collection of all the files that Git is tracking for your particular project.

As you work, you add your changes to *stage,* a temporary space that tracks the files, using the command git add [*filename, foldername,* or -A for all files]. When you're ready to finalize things, you *commit* your changes to the branch using the command git commit -m "*message goes here*".

Origin is your remote repository, where you push and pull all the working code for your project. This is generally a repository that is saved on GitHub or a similar Git-enabled hosting service.

Setting Up Git for Your Workflow

For a solo workflow, I'll typically start with three clones of the same repository:

- A remote *Origin*, hosted on GitHub.
- A local clone of the repository, hosted on my MAMP server.
- A second remote clone, hosted on a staging server with protected access. The staging server allows clients and collaborators to view the site's progress as it's happening, without affecting the production (i.e. live/launch) domain.

All of these repositories are *clones* of each other, which means they have the same files and data; *pushing* and *pulling* syncs the files among them. Most development workflows will typically start this way; as you add collaborators, or move your code from staging to launch, each of these different environments will require its own clone of the main repository. Each collaborator on the team will *push* and *pull* to the main repository.

---

1. For more on branches, check out this great writeup on version control: *http://hoth.entp.com/output/git _for_designers.html*.

When I first started using Git, I was overwhelmed by trying to figure out how everything worked. After a few times, however, I realized it was relatively easy to get the hang of. The basic workflow is this:

1. Create an empty repository on GitHub, which will become *Origin*.

2. Create a local directory for your installation and copy your files into it.

3. In Terminal.app, navigate to the new directory and initialize your new *Master*:

   ```
   git init;
   ```

4. Commit your files to *Master* by typing the following:

   ```
   git add -A
   git commit -m "first commit"
   ```

5. Add the remote *Origin* you just created on GitHub using the command:

   ```
   git remote add origin git@github.com/USERNAME/REPOSITORY-NAME.git;
   ```

6. Push the files to GitHub using the following:

   ```
   git push origin master
   ```

Next, we'll look at those steps in a bit more detail. Steps 1–4 cover installation, and only need to be done once per computer you're installing Git on. The rest of the steps will help you set up the workflow for each project.

Step 1: Create an SSH Key

In order to push your first commit to the remote *Origin* you'll create in step 2, you'll need to create an SSH key for your account. This helps your computer connect securely to GitHub, and you only need to do it once per computer you want to access the repository from. The GitHub site has a pretty in-depth writeup of how to do this at *http://help.github.com/mac-set-up-git/*; however, I'll give you the basic steps here.

1. In Terminal.app, navigate to your ssh directory using the command:

   ```
   cd ~/.ssh
   ```

2. Check to see what's in the directory by using the command:

   ```
   ls
   ```

3. This will list all the contents of the directory. If you see the filenames *id_rsa* and *id_rsa.pub*, those are your current SSH keys; you can skip to 5 on page 30. If you don't see them, you want to create a new one. To generate a new SSH key, enter the code:

   ```
   ssh-keygen -t rsa -C "your_email@youremail.com"
   Enter file in which to save the key (/Users/your_user_directory/.ssh/id_rsa):
   ```

4. Now you need to enter a passphrase.

   ```
   Enter passphrase (empty for no passphrase):<enter a passphrase>
   Enter same passphrase again:<enter passphrase again>
   ```

This should give you a message like this:

```
Your identification has been saved in /Users/your_user_directory/.ssh/id_rsa.
Your public key has been saved in /Users/your_user_directory/.ssh/id_rsa.pub.

The key fingerprint is:
01:0f:f4:3b:ca:85:d6:17:a1:7d:f0:68:9d:f0:a2:db user_name@username.com
```

5. You now want to add this key to your GitHub account.

 If you don't have a GitHub account yet, skip to "Step 4: Set Up a GitHub Account" on page 33 for a moment and come back.

To do this, go into the Account Settings page and click the SSH Public Keys tab (see Figure 4-1). Create a new key by pressing the Add a New Key button.

Figure 4-1. Adding our SSH key to GitHub

Now you have to get the contents of your actual RSA key. If you have your Finder set up to show hidden files (this is usually not a good idea, as it's easy to accidentally delete things you need), you can navigate directly to the *.ssh* directory and open *id_rsa.pub* in a text editor like TextWrangler to copy the key. Personally, I prefer using the command line. Assuming that you're still in the *~/.ssh* directory (if you aren't, use `cd ~/.ssh` to navigate there now) you can use the following code to spit out the key:

```
ls
```

This spits out the contents of the directory, which should be:

```
id_rsa id_rsa.pub known_hosts
```

From there, type the following code:

```
cat id_rsa.pub
```

It should spit out a long line of gobbledygook that starts with `ssh-rsa` and ends with your email address. Copy all of it with no lines or extra spaces and paste it into the text box on GitHub, then click Add Key. Go ahead; I'll wait.

Once you do that, you should be all set to `push` and `pull` to your GitHub account.

Step 2: Install Git

Installing Git is fairly straightforward, although it does require you to step into the command Line.l

To install Git, the first thing you need to do is grab the installer. To do this, visit git-scm.com and download the installer appropriate to your OS. Find the icon that suits your operating system (see the box on the right in Figure 4-2), and use it to download the right installer.

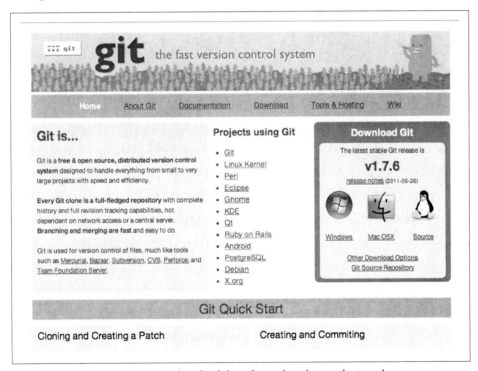

Figure 4-2. Installing Git. You can download the software by selecting the icon that represents your operating system.

Install the Git software using the instructions that come with the package you downloaded. Once it's installed, if you go into Terminal.app (on the Mac) and type `git`, you should see a whole bunch of commands in the window (see Figure 4-3). If it doesn't work, try quitting Terminal.app and re-opening it.

```
Danielles-MacBook-Air:homesteaders Dani$ git
usage: git [--version] [--exec-path[=<path>]] [--html-path] [--man-path] [--info-p
ath]
           [-p|--paginate|--no-pager] [--no-replace-objects]
           [--bare] [--git-dir=<path>] [--work-tree=<path>]
           [-c name=value] [--help]
           <command> [<args>]

The most commonly used git commands are:
   add        Add file contents to the index
   bisect     Find by binary search the change that introduced a bug
   branch     List, create, or delete branches
   checkout   Checkout a branch or paths to the working tree
   clone      Clone a repository into a new directory
   commit     Record changes to the repository
   diff       Show changes between commits, commit and working tree, etc
   fetch      Download objects and refs from another repository
   grep       Print lines matching a pattern
   init       Create an empty git repository or reinitialize an existing one
   log        Show commit logs
   merge      Join two or more development histories together
   mv         Move or rename a file, a directory, or a symlink
   pull       Fetch from and merge with another repository or a local branch
   push       Update remote refs along with associated objects
   rebase     Forward-port local commits to the updated upstream head
   reset      Reset current HEAD to the specified state
   rm         Remove files from the working tree and from the index
   show       Show various types of objects
   status     Show the working tree status
   tag        Create, list, delete or verify a tag object signed with GPG

See 'git help <command>' for more information on a specific command.
```

Figure 4-3. The Git manual, as seen from Terminal

Once you've installed Git, you also want to set up some configurations within your specific installation. This helps make it easier to see what's been checked out and in by whom, which is especially useful if you're collaborating with others.

Step 3: Set Up Your Git Configuration

Type the following into Terminal to navigate to the *.ssh* directory:

```
cd ~/.ssh
```

If you don't have an *.ssh* directory (which sometimes happens), you can create it:

```
mkdir ~/.ssh
chmod 700 ~/.ssh
```

mkdir creates the directory, while chmod 700 makes sure that only your user—i.e., YOU—has access to that directory (important for the security of your system).

Type the following into your Terminal (within the *.ssh* folder) to set up your Git configuration:

```
git config --global user.name "First Last"
git config --global user.email "username@example.com"
git config --global color.ui true
git config --global color.status auto
git config --global color.branch auto
git config --global color.interactive auto
git config --global color.diff auto
```

Then type the following into Terminal:

```
git config -l --global
```

Now you'll see your configuration settings. The above configuration gives Git records as to who made the commit that you've posted, and it gives you the ability to read the Git commands more easily by color coding them.

Step 4: Set Up a GitHub Account

I use GitHub to store my remote repositories. GitHub is fairly easy to set up, and it's reasonably priced (free if you make all your repositories public; $7/month if you want to have up to five private repositories and a few collaborators—important for client work; there are additional plans available as well). Once you have an account and sign in, the GitHub Dashboard (see Figure 4-4) has instructions on how to create a repository and do some other common things you'll need to do on GitHub. Go ahead, poke around; I'll wait.

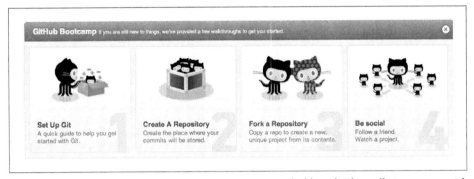

Figure 4-4. The GitHubBootcamp screen on your account dashboard. This will give you a quick overview of what you need to know.

Step 5: Create the Remote Repository

Once you have your account set up, the first step is to create a repository. For client projects, I keep my repositories private. I prefer not to have my code hanging around where other people can grab at it. To create a new repository, click the "New Repository" button on your GitHub dashboard (see Figure 4-5).

Figure 4-5. Creating a new repository (Image borrowed from http://help.github.com/create-a-repo/)

In the screen that follows (see Figure 4-6), give the repository a name and description, and choose whether you want it to be private or public.

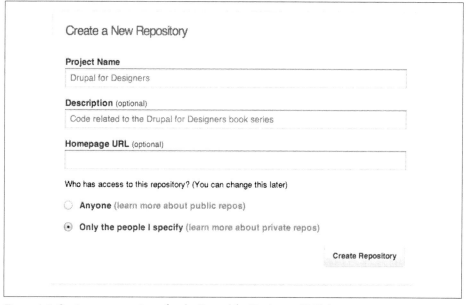

Figure 4-6. Setting up a repository for the Drupal for Designers GitHub project

Step 6: Set Up the Local Repository

Once you have your repository set up on GitHub, you'll get a set of instructions on the next screen that walks you through the commands you need to create a local repository on your computer. This will help you set up Git so that your code can synchronize between your local and remote repositories.

To create your local repository, you want to start by going into the folder that holds your Drupal installation. This, as we may recall, is done using the following:

```
cd ~/path/to/d7-demo
```

Once you're there, use the following commands to start a local repository, make your first commit, add a remote repository, and push your files to the remote repository.

```
git init
git add -A
git commit -m "first commit"
git remote add origin git@github.com:USERNAME/REPOSITORY-NAME.git
git push origin master
```

Do all of those things in Terminal.app, using the values for your GitHub account name and the name of your repository. Once you've created your remote *Origin*, use the git pull command to pull down the changes on the remote server each time you start doing work, and use git push to push the changes back once you're done.

So What Happens on a Team?

The instructions above will help you set up a *Master* repository on your local machine, and push it to a remote *Origin* account. But what happens if you're working on a team? Or you want to have a version of the code on a staging server? This is where things get fun.

First Things First: The Git Workflow

Assuming that you're developing locally (you are developing locally, aren't you?), your workflow would look like this:

1. At the start of your coding session, use the following code in Terminal.app to navigate to your project folder and pull the latest code from the repository:

   ```
   cd ~/PATH/TO/FOLDER
   git pull
   ```

2. As you work, use this code to add your changes to Git for tracking and commit them to the *Master* repository:

   ```
   git add [FILENAME, DIRECTORY or -A]
   git commit -m "Description of Changes"
   ```

3. When you're finished, or ready to show your changes to the team, do one last pull:

   ```
   git pull
   ```

   Then push your changes back into the *Origin* repository by using the following:

   ```
   git push
   ```

4. If you have a second version of the repository hosted on a staging server, you'd then log into the staging server via SSH and use `git pull` to pull the changes down into the staging server.

 Why pull before pushing? You may have noticed that in step 3, we pulled from *Origin* before we pushed back to it. This is important when you have more than one person working on a repository, and it's a good habit to get into. Pulling the code down syncs any changes that have been made by your other collaborators with the code you're working on; pushing the code adds all the changes back to *Origin*.

And There We Go

So now we've set up a local development environment, installed Drush, downloaded some modules, and set up Git for our project. Next, we'll talk about two additional bits of awesomeness that you can add to your Drupal toolkit to make life easier: Features and Drush Make files.

PART II

Using Features and Drush Make to Make Development Easier

CHAPTER 5

Using Features in Your Workflow

Along the way, you (like me) might find that many of the sites you work on tend to have the same general sections. You'll have an events section, some testimonials, a blog, or some other type of functionality that always turns out pretty much the same way.

Or, let's say that you're one of a team of folks working on a specific project. You're plugging away at a local copy of the site, updating a View so that you can correctly theme it...when you realize that none of the changes you just made to the View will translate to the site that everyone else is working on.

Enter Features. Features is a Drupal module that allows you to pack up specific chunks of functionality—content types, views, etc.—and export it as a custom module that you can then install on any site you want.

Let's look at the first example: commonly built functionality. My site, and many other sites I've done, usually include some sort of events page. Each event has a date and time, a location, title, and description, as well as a link to register for the event or learn more at an external website. Once the content type was created and content was entered, you create a View that will populate the Events page, and maybe include a block display for the sidebar.

In order to create this section, you do each task separately, with each task taking anywhere from half an hour to several, depending on the complexity. With Features, you can create it once, export it as a feature, and install that feature on any number of sites.

To start working with Features, you want to download and install the Features module (drupal.org/project/features). You also want to install Strongarm (drupal.org/project/strongarm), which will help you maintain the configurations of your feature (particularly important for including content types).

For our Events feature, we create:

- An Event content type, with several custom fields.
- An Events view, with upcoming events as one (page) display, an events archive as an (attachment) display, and a block display that features a list of events for a sidebar listing.

Once you have everything set up the way you want it, go to the Features panel by clicking Structure→Features. You will soon arrive at a screen similar to that of Figure 5-1:

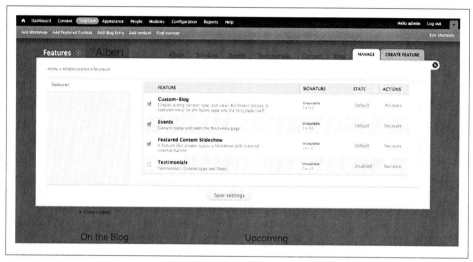

Figure 5-1. The Features Window on a Drupal 7 site build. Note that some features have already been created and installed.

To create your feature, click the Create Feature tab. This will give you a screen like the one in Figure 5-2.

In the first set of fields, you set up your feature defaults. We'll call this one Events, and give it a description of "Creates an event content type and views for an events listing." In the Version field, give it a version of 7.x-1.0 (meaning it's a Drupal 7 feature, and this is the first iteration of it). It's important not to leave those first three fields empty; they help create the *.info* file for your new custom module.

Below that first set of fields, you're going to start adding in the functionality for your feature. Start by adding the content type. Under Components, select Content Types and choose the Event content type. Now that you've added your content type, from the Components list, choose Strongarm and choose every element that relates to your Event content type. You can usually find them by doing a search on the page for the name of the content type, e.g. "event".

Figure 5-2. Setting up our Feature description

Finally, choose Views from the Components list and choose the view you created for your Events section. If your work depends on a specific contributed module, like Semantic Fields or Display Suite, and it didn't show up in the Dependencies section, you also want to add those under Dependencies in the Components list.

By the end of all this work, you should have something that looks like Figure 5-3.

Once all your components are assembled, you can download your feature by clicking the Download Feature button. Your feature will download as a *.tar.gz* file, which you can unpack and install into a custom directory under your *sites/all/modules* folder. Once it's in that folder, you can enable the feature under either the Modules list or by returning to Structure→Features.

What features do, essentially, is turn your database configurations (in the form of content type, views, variables, etc.) into module code. This is fantastic when you want something that works out of the box—but what if you want to change the default settings of your new feature? How do you make edits without destroying the feature?

That, my friend, is the best thing about Features.

Let's go back to our Event content type. Looking at the block I created on my homepage, it looks like Figure 5-4.

It looks beautiful, but I realized that I want "Link to Page" to say "Learn More" instead. Since the "Link to Page" label is part of my Events View, I can go into that display, change the label of the Link to Page field to Learn More, and save the View. Now my display looks like Figure 5-5.

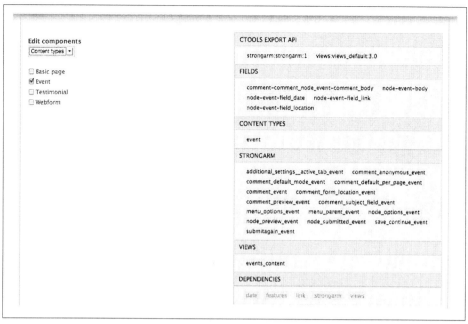

Figure 5-3. Your finished components list. In addition to what's here, you can also include specific modules required by your content types, such as Fieldgroup.

But if we return to our Features tab (see Figure 5-6), we'll notice that the Events feature we just created has been overridden by the database.

When you override a feature, it's important to make sure that you update the code. The reason for this is twofold. First, if you're using the feature as part of a development workflow (for example, you're developing the site locally, but have to push changes to the server), updating the feature's code and pushing it to your remote server gives you the opportunity to transfer the changes from your local site to the remote site with relative ease. Second, updating the code keeps you safe against potential problems with your database down the road.

There are two ways to update your features. One way is to recreate the feature using the Recreate link on the Features page. Download the feature again, and replace the code in your *sites/all/modules/custom* folder. Refresh the page, and everything's all set.

The other way to do it, which is much quicker, is on the command line. Features comes with a set of Drush commands specific to managing Features:

drush features
> Gives you a list of all the Features installed on your site.

drush features-update *FEATURE_NAME*
> Updates code for a feature that has been overridden by the database.

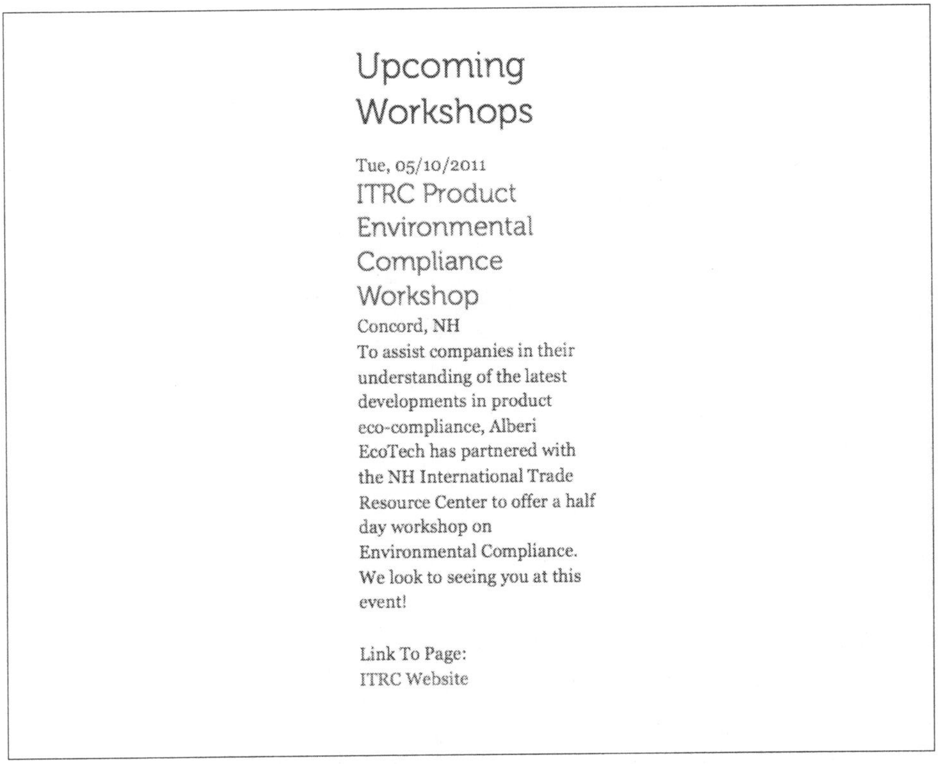

Upcoming Workshops

Tue, 05/10/2011
ITRC Product Environmental Compliance Workshop

Concord, NH
To assist companies in their understanding of the latest developments in product eco-compliance, Alberi EcoTech has partnered with the NH International Trade Resource Center to offer a half day workshop on Environmental Compliance. We look to seeing you at this event!

Link To Page:
ITRC Website

Figure 5-4. Our Upcoming Workshops block, built from one of the Views displays in our Feature

```
drush features-revert FEATURE_NAME
```
Reverts a feature that has been overridden by the database back to the original code.

Remember, all of these commands should be used from inside your Drupal installation. In Figure 5-7, you'll notice that I used `drush features-update events` to update my Events feature.

In my short time working with Features on my own sites, I've seen both benefits and challenges to this workflow. The biggest benefit to this workflow is both its portability and speed. Developing locally, frankly, saves time; you don't have to worry about waiting for an FTP server to accept your file, or about accidentally uploading the wrong file and wondering how to get it back. Additionally, since working in Drupal is so often a dance between configuration in the database and tinkering with code, Features allows you to get this same speed on your local machine without having to worry (too much) about syncing a database between your local and remote machines.

Speaking of syncing a database, it's important to note that Features won't export the *content* in your work to code. As such, if you're using Features to prototype something that involves a number of content types or complex node relationships, you'll still have

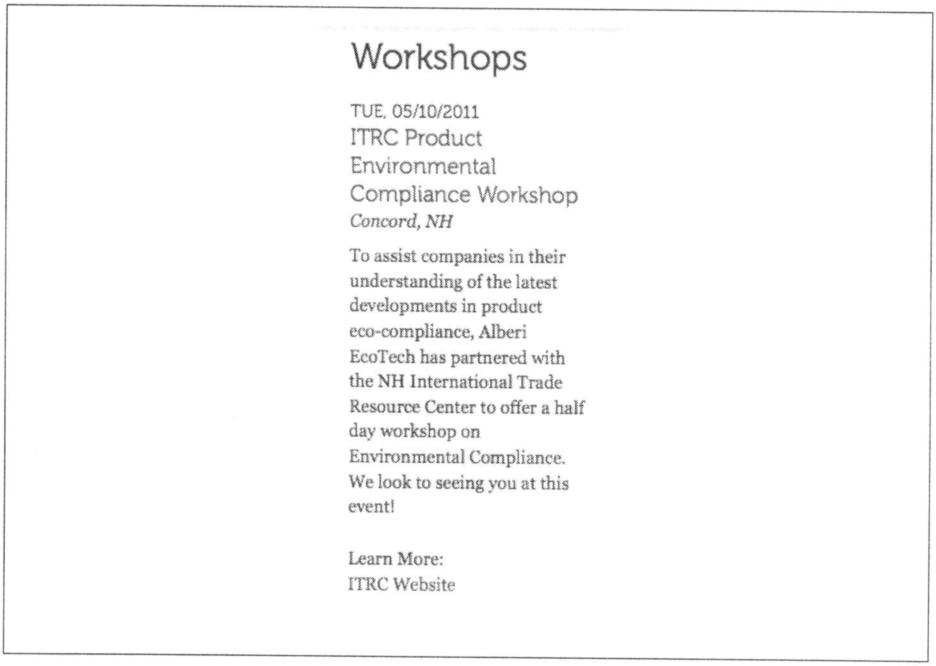

Workshops

TUE, 05/10/2011
ITRC Product
Environmental
Compliance Workshop
Concord, NH

To assist companies in their
understanding of the latest
developments in product
eco-compliance, Alberi
EcoTech has partnered with
the NH International Trade
Resource Center to offer a half
day workshop on
Environmental Compliance.
We look to seeing you at this
event!

Learn More:
ITRC Website

Figure 5-5. Our Views display, fixed up a bit

to recreate any content you added on your local machine when you install or update the Feature. This, in fact, is the one case where it might make more sense to sync databases back and forth instead of using Features; during one project, I ended up having to recreate about 30 pieces of content on the staging site after updating my Feature, which was officially Not Fun.

Still More Awesomeness Awaits

So far, we've learned a bunch of new ways to protect your work and make your life as a Drupal designer easier. As we inch towards the finish line, we're going to talk about my absolute favorite Drupal development trick: the Drush *.make* file. With this one file, you can use Drush to download Drupal, including any contrib or custom modules, themes, or libraries you want—even a custom install profile—within about five minutes.

Figure 5-6. When you change an aspect of a Feature, the feature shows as Overridden in the listing

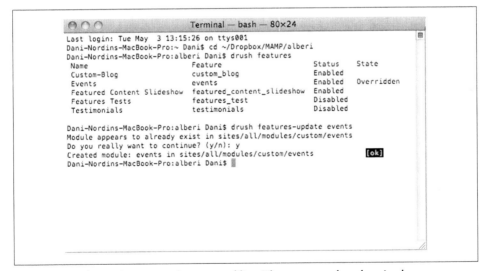

Figure 5-7. Updating Features on the command line. Three commands and you're done.

CHAPTER 6

Making Drupal Easier: Working with Drush Make and Installation Profiles

As you continue working in Drupal, you'll likely notice that you use certain modules again and again. Normally, you'd start off a project by downloading and enabling each module manually; you may even end up compiling, as I did for a while, a checklist of modules that belong on every project. While a checklist is a convenient way to remember all the modules you typically use, it still takes time to download and install them. Even using Drush to do it can get monotonous at times—and if you're doing a lot of modules, it's easy to make a mistake and type the wrong filename. And while you could also create a local installation that serves as a "base install" with all your configurations, it takes time and effort to keep the code and modules updated in the base installation, and creating a new site requires not only copying those files into a new folder, but copying the database as well. It's not the worst workflow, but it's not the most efficient either.

What if there was a way for you to run a script that would download Drupal for you, download all your modules and base themes, and basically create your file structure for you so you can get to work on configuring modules and designing something awesome? That's what Drush Make is for. Drush Make is an extension for Drush that will allow you to specify:

- Which core version you want to download (e.g. 6.x or 7.x)
- Which modules you want
- Which base theme you'd like
- Any external libraries or other bits of code you want

And *download it all to the folder you're in*. Combine this with an installation profile that enables the modules you want, sets your base theme as the new default, and establishes other key settings, and you can have a new site up and running within about 15 to 30 minutes—with many of your most commonly used defaults already set up.

Step 1: Install Drush Make

To start using Drush Make, you first need to install the extension. It's best to do this in a hidden directory in your home folder, rather than in the *drush* directory. The reason for this is simple—at some point, you may end up upgrading Drush. If you do, and Drush Make is in the main */drush* directory, you've just deleted Drush Make.

1. Download the project from drupal.org/project/drush_make.

2. Unpack the *tar.gz* file into your working folder (again, this is your home folder).

3. Move the folder into a hidden directory called *.drush*. Start by navigating to your home directory using `cd ~`.

4. Then make a hidden *.drush* directory: `mkdir .drush`.

5. Finally, move the *drush_make* folder into your new hidden directory: `mv drush_make ~/.drush`.

Now, you need to create a *.make* file for it to run. If you go back to the project page for Drush Make, you'll find a sample *.make* file under the "Documentation and Resources" heading called *EXAMPLE.make*. Copy the text from that file and paste it into a new file in your favorite text editor (I'm using Coda, but you can also use TextWrangler for Mac or a similar free text editor). Now, you can start customizing it any way you want.

Each *.make* file starts with specifying the version of Drupal core that you're working with and the Drush Make API version. I like to include comments in my files to help organize, which are preceded by a semicolon:

```
; Specify Drupal core and Drush API version
core = 7.x
api = 2
```

Then you want to specify the actual Core project (aka Drupal core):

```
; Core project
projects[] = drupal
```

Now, you want to specify the modules you want to download.

 Drush Make will only download versions of modules that are compatible with the version of Drupal you're specifying, and those that have current recommended releases. This means that, while I'd normally include semantic_fields in my "Theming Helpers" section, I can't because it's not in recommended release yet. You can still use Drush to download the module, however, once the *.make* file finishes running.

I like to group modules by what they're used for, or by a specific dependency, with comments. For example, I'll just start with Views, Ctools, Pathauto, and Token, which are common to most Drupal installations:

```
; Standard modules
projects[] = views
projects[] = ctools
projects[] = pathauto
projects[] = token
```

Then I'll add some of my favorite theming helper modules, and the WYSIWYG module, with its dependency, Libraries:

```
; Theming helpers
projects[] = block_class

; WYSIWYG
projects[] = wysiwyg
projects[] = libraries
```

Then I'll add my base theme, Omega:

```
; Base theme
projects[] = omega
```

Now, I'll save the file as *make_basic.make*, and save it in a *makefiles* directory in my home folder. Here's where the magic happens.

Let's say that now I want to create a new Drupal installation for a client project. I'll start in Terminal.app by navigating to my MAMP folder and creating a new directory for the project. We'll call it *make-test* for now.

```
cd ~/Dropbox/MAMP
mkdir make-test
```

Now, I'll navigate into my new folder and call my *make_basic.make* file using Drush.

```
cd make-test
drush make ~/makefiles/make_basic.make
y
y
```

When we're done, we'll see something approximating Figure 6-1 in Terminal.

```
Danielles-MacBook-Air:.drush Dani$ cd ~
Danielles-MacBook-Air:~ Dani$ cd Dropbox/MAMP
Danielles-MacBook-Air:MAMP Dani$ mkdir make-test
Danielles-MacBook-Air:MAMP Dani$ cd make-test
Danielles-MacBook-Air:make-test Dani$ drush make ~/makefiles/make_basic.make
Make new site in the current directory? (y/n): y
Project information for drupal retrieved.                         [ok]
Project information for views retrieved.                          [ok]
Project information for ctools retrieved.                         [ok]
drupal downloaded from                                            [ok]
http://ftp.drupal.org/files/projects/drupal-7.7.tar.gz.
views downloaded from                                            [ok]
http://ftp.drupal.org/files/projects/views-7.x-3.0-rc1.tar.gz.
ctools downloaded from                                            [ok]
http://ftp.drupal.org/files/projects/ctools-7.x-1.0-beta1.tar.gz.
Make new site in the current directory? (y/n): y
Danielles-MacBook-Air:make-test Dani$ ▉
```

Figure 6-1. Drush Make downloading all of the modules and stuff that we need for our Drupal installation

And if we go back into the Finder and navigate to our new *make-test* directory, we'll see something like Figure 6-2.

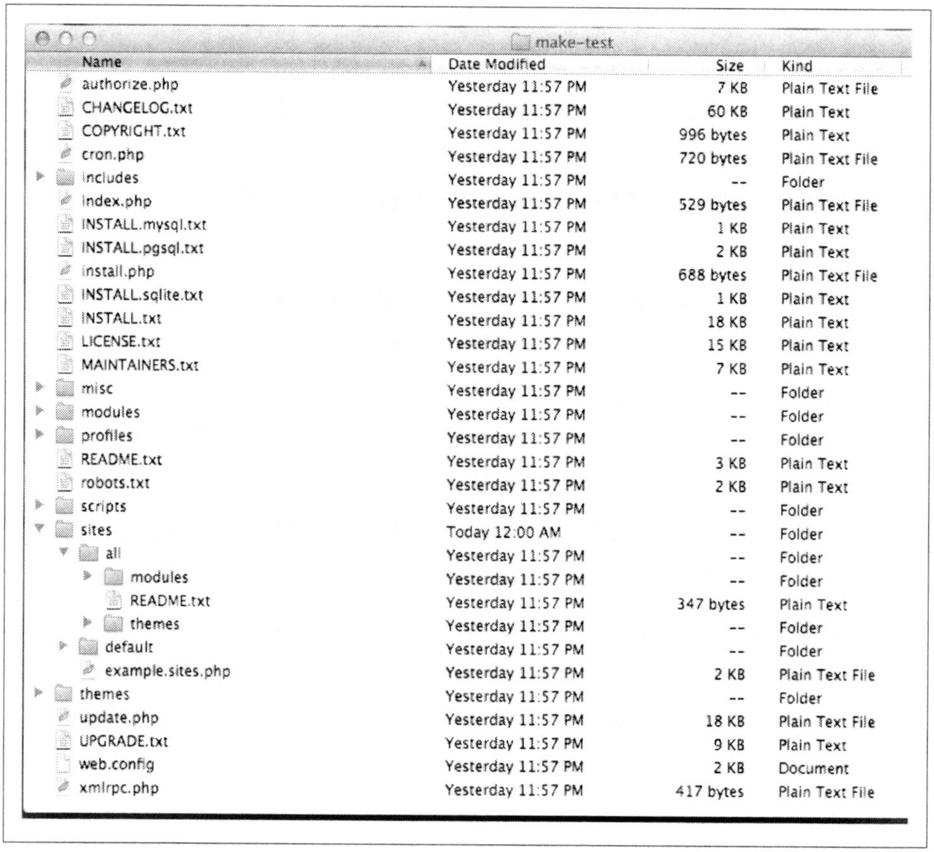

Figure 6-2. In about a minute, we just downloaded our entire Drupal installation, a base theme and the modules we need to get started, in the right locations. Sweet!

Why This Is Lovely

If you've done Drupal sites for any length of time, you will likely notice that there are certain modules—or a specific base theme—that you return to over and over again. Using .make files, you can set up a file to download everything you need for a specific use case—say, a standard promotional corporate site, or a web community—and running that one file will download everything you need to get started *in about five minutes.*

Getting Started with Install Profiles

Once you've got a *.make* file ready, with all of the modules and other things that you typically use for a project, you may want to make your life even easier by creating an install profile that enables all of your modules for you, and sets up a few of the configurations that you have to reset over and over again. Although install profiles can be tricky to set up, they can be huge time savers. While the *.make* file does the hard work of downloading and unpacking most of your modules for you, the install profile can be set up to actually enable all of those modules, along with a host of other things, like:

- Setting up default user roles and permissions (such as *editor, administrator*, and other commonly needed user roles)
- Setting up appropriate input formats (like adding <h1>–<h4> tags and the like)
- Populating the database with some sample content
- And much more!

In Drupal 7, profiles are set up like modules, and need the following to work:

- A *profilename.info* file that sets up your dependencies (the modules that are enabled when the profile is used to install Drupal)
- A *profilename.install* file that actually installs Drupal for you
- A *profilename.profile* file that sets up your configurations for you

The documentation for install profiles at *http://drupal.org/node/1022020* provides a great starting point for making your own install profile. I like to start my new profile by copying and modifying the Standard profile that comes with Drupal 7 core (located in the *profiles* folder). It should also be noted that, for certain things, like a specific configuration of content types and Views (like an Events section, or a News section), you're better off packing it up into Features, which we talked about in Chapter 5.

So Here We Are

In this relatively slim volume, we've managed to set up a local development environment, learn the basics of Drush, Git, and some command line fu, and we've discovered how to make our lives as designers and site builders easier using Features and Drush Make. I won't pretend that some of this stuff isn't annoying; indeed, we've only scratched the surface of what's possible with all of this stuff. But, if you're willing to give it a shot, these tools can make your life infinitely easier as a Drupal designer—and free you to focus your attention on more important priorities, such as creating design that will wow your clients and get people's attention.

Use these tools in good health; and remember that for every headache you end up with during your site building adventures, I—and the entire Drupal community—will be here to cheer you on.

About the Author

Dani Nordin is an independent user experience designer and strategist who specializes in smart, human-friendly design for progressive brands. She discovered design purely by accident as a Theatre student at Rhode Island College in 1995, and has been doing some combination of design, public speaking, and writing ever since.

Dani is a regular feature at Boston's Drupal meetup, and is a regular speaker at Boston's Design for Drupal Camp. In 2011, she was one of several contributors to *The Definitive Guide to Drupal 7*, published by Apress; *Drupal for Designers* is her second book. You can check out some of her work at *tzk-design.com*. She also blogs almost regularly at *daninordin.com*.

Dani lives in Watertown, MA, with her husband Nick and Persephone, a 14-pound ~~giant ball of black furry love~~ cat. Both are infinite sources of comedic gold.

Get even more for your money.

Join the O'Reilly Community, and register the O'Reilly books you own. It's free, and you'll get:

- $4.99 ebook upgrade offer
- 40% upgrade offer on O'Reilly print books
- Membership discounts on books and events
- Free lifetime updates to ebooks and videos
- Multiple ebook formats, DRM FREE
- Participation in the O'Reilly community
- Newsletters
- Account management
- 100% Satisfaction Guarantee

Signing up is easy:

1. **Go to: oreilly.com/go/register**
2. **Create an O'Reilly login.**
3. **Provide your address.**
4. **Register your books.**

Note: English-language books only

To order books online:
oreilly.com/store

For questions about products or an order:
orders@oreilly.com

To sign up to get topic-specific email announcements and/or news about upcoming books, conferences, special offers, and new technologies:
elists@oreilly.com

For technical questions about book content:
booktech@oreilly.com

To submit new book proposals to our editors:
proposals@oreilly.com

O'Reilly books are available in multiple DRM-free ebook formats. For more information:
oreilly.com/ebooks

O'REILLY®

Spreading the knowledge of innovators   oreilly.com

Have it your way.

CPSIA information can be obtained at www.ICGtesting.com
Printed in the USA
BVOW081428230312

285915BV00001B/1/P